DEDICATION

*To my daughter, Ashley, who leads with her heart in
everything she does. She never lets her head get in the way of her heart.*

*Although Ashley has Down syndrome, and has an IQ
of only 36, she has taught me much more than I've taught her.*

*Also dedicated to those wonderful people who take
full responsibility for their relationships—who have attained a balance
between their heads and hearts—and thereby truly live the prayer,*

"Let there be peace on Earth and let it begin with me."

AL RITTER

THE

100/0

PRINCIPLE

THE SECRET OF
GREAT RELATIONSHIPS

Published by Simple Truths, LLC
1952 McDowell Road
Naperville, Illinois 60563
800-900-3427
www.simpletruths.com

Written with Help From: Stephanie Trannel

Design and production: Jared McDaniel, Studio430.com

Printed and bound in the United States of America

ISBN 978-1-60810-070-5

05 WOZ 12

CONTENTS

INTRODUCTION

"I present myself to you in a form suitable to the
relationship I wish to achieve with you."

LUIGI PIRANDELLO

RELATIONSHIPS SURROUND US, CONFOUND US, *and sometimes* LEAD TO OUR DEFEAT.

We're immersed in them 24/7. At home, at work and everywhere in between, each encounter with another person is a relationship in which we can present our best self . . . or not. The truth is, good, effective relationships make almost everything more enjoyable and more advantageous.

Think about the way you interact with others, about the way you approach relationships; about your expectations and assumptions. Are you unconsciously sabotaging yourself? Are you standing in the way of your own success?

This book aims to help you recognize certain relationship pitfalls, learn how to overcome them, and make every relationship great. Not only will you enjoy this book, but our prediction is it will significantly, and fairly easily, change your life for the better!

Written for all members of the human race, no matter your role in this world, or for that matter, your age; **you will gain a clear way to improve your personal and professional effectiveness.**

Is your relationship with others based primarily on your judgment of them, either positive or negative? If you answered "yes," thank you for being honest. The truth, for most of us, is that our treatment of other people is derived from our judgment of them, that is, whether we perceive them as right or wrong; whether we agree or disagree with them.

Sometimes the tendency to judge others is appropriate. We want to be able to accurately assess others in situations such as the hiring process, giving performance reviews, and being alert to problematic people, to name just a few.

There are many other times, however, when our tendency to judge creates a great disservice to ourselves and others. When it comes to family, friends, coworkers and customers, our relationship is more important (in fact, much more important) than our assessment of how right or wrong the other person is. In these circumstances, it behooves us to take 100% responsibility for the relationship, expecting nothing in return.

The genesis of this book comes from 20-plus years of coaching, consulting, writing and speaking. I have learned that the most effective people at all levels and in all walks of life take full advantage of *The 100/0 Principle*. And you can too.

Would you rather be *right*, or would you rather be *happy and effective?*

AS YOU READ THIS BOOK

I am often asked to provide people with tips that will help them implement *The 100/0 Principle* in their organizations and lives. As you read this book, there are two keys you must keep in mind: AWARENESS and CHOICE. By having an awareness of your natural tendency to react to someone, you'll be able to make a **choice** to respond in a more effective—often counterintuitive—manner.

A TYPICAL REACTION:

Automatic, reactive and judgment based

Consequence: *often unsatisfactory and ineffective*

AN ALTERNATE RESPONSE:

Thoughtful, aware and choice based

Consequence: *usually satisfactory and effective*

Train yourself to be *aware* of your automatic, judgmental tendencies, then consciously and intentionally *choose* how to respond.

The overall challenge is to determine who is in charge: Are your automatic thoughts/judgments in charge, or are **you** in charge of your responses? I have a choice, you have a choice, we all have a choice. Our effectiveness in relationships is based on our ability to be in charge; to take personal responsibility for how we respond to other people.

"Some of the biggest challenges in relationships come from the fact that most people enter a relationship in order to get something: They're trying to find someone who's going to make them feel good. In reality, the only way a relationship will last is if you see your relationship as a place that you go to give, and not a place you go to take."

— Anthony Robbins —

CHAPTER 1

ACTION + RE

"Eighty percent of life's satisfaction

comes from meaningful relationships."

BRIAN TRACY

LATIONSHIPS
= RESULTS

Most of us know that our relationships with others are important. Many people spend more time at work than anywhere else, making the need for solid relationships necessary. We know that our relationships with our parents, our kids and our friends sustain us and are essential to our well-being.

However, many of us don't appreciate another aspect of relationships—**the strength of our relationships, combined with the actions we take, determine the results we achieve**—in all domains of our lives. Thus, a powerful formula for success is:

> ### ACTIONS + RELATIONSHIPS = RESULTS

In our work with thousands of leaders and teams the past 20 years, we have come to fully appreciate the importance of relationships in any worthwhile endeavor. In fact, we have found that **an equal commitment to both actions and relationships, never compromising one for the other, is the big key to success.** Most of us see clearly the connection between action and results. What we don't see as clearly is the connection between relationships and results.

How many opportunities have you missed to produce real, unprecedented, breakthrough results when you were committed to taking action, but were less committed to, or even unaware of, **the critical importance of relationships in achieving those results?**

This book is about a simple, yet profound way for you to create powerful relationships with other people, and thereby help you achieve what you want in all domains of your life:

work

family

community

social

spiritual

financial

and recreational.

A LESSON ON RELATIONSHIPS FROM THE GREAT COACHES

Some years ago, we were fortunate to work directly with two of the universally acknowledged great coaches in American sports: Red Auerbach, former coach of the Boston Celtics and winner of nine NBA championships, and John Wooden, former coach at UCLA and winner of 10 NCAA championships. We asked them the secret to their masterful success. Their answers to our question were quite revealing:

"Most average, and even good, coaches have a clear commitment to winning (results). We, on the other hand, also had that commitment to winning, but we had an equal commitment to rapport and chemistry (relationship), and we never compromised one for the other. That's what made us and our teams successful."

We have taken that lesson from the great coaches to all our clients, and have never seen that concept fail, no matter the specific situation. And as we've learned, *The 100/0 Principle* is the quickest and most effective way to fulfill the commitment to powerful relationships.

THE BOTTOM LINE

In a nutshell, we all want to achieve our goals in life, whether for our family, our organization, our team or for ourselves. And most of us want to achieve significant or unprecedented results in one or more of those life domains.

> THE RELATIONSHIPS WE CREATE
> ARE ABSOLUTELY CRITICAL
> TO OUR SUCCESS.

What's not so obvious is the essential role of *The 100/0 Principle* in creating and sustaining our relationships.

Taking full responsibility for a relationship . . . it's so simple that we will miss it if we don't pay careful attention. Its simple truth is accompanied, for most of us, by some difficulty since carrying it out requires counterintuitive thinking and action. It requires that you and I treat other people with dignity and respect even when we think they don't deserve it, and even when people around us say they don't deserve it.

Relate to It

LAST TIME YOU STRUGGLED TO REACH A GOAL, WHAT RELATIONSHIP OBSTACLES WERE IN YOUR WAY?

HOW COULD YOU HAVE USED **THE 100/0 PRINCIPLE** TO REACH YOUR GOAL?

The 100/0 Principle is the simplest, most direct and most effective way to create solid relationships.

"Life is an echo—
WHAT YOU SEND OUT COMES BACK."

CHINESE PROVERB

2

How

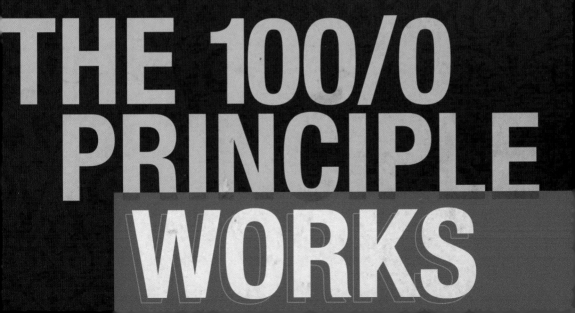

> *"When you are tempted to judge,*
> *remember we are all ONE."*

UNKNOWN

THE 100/0
PRINCIPLE
WORKS

What is the most effective way to create and sustain great relationships with others? As you know by now, it's *The 100/0 Principle*: You take full responsibility (the 100) for the relationship, expecting nothing (the 0) in return.

Implementing *The 100/0 Principle* is not natural for most of us. It takes real commitment to the relationship and a good dose of self-discipline to think, act and give 100 percent.

The 100/0 Principle applies to those people in your life where the relationships are too important to react automatically or judgmentally. Each of us must determine the relationships to which this principle should apply. For most of us, it applies to work associates, customers, suppliers, family and friends.

STEP 1 Determine what you can do to make the relationship work … then do it. Demonstrate respect and kindness to the other person, whether he/she deserves it or not.

STEP 2 Do not expect anything in return. Zero, zip, nada.

STEP 3 Do not allow anything the other person says or does (no matter how annoying!) to affect you. In other words, don't take the bait.

STEP 4 Be persistent with your graciousness and kindness. Often we give up too soon, especially when others don't respond in kind. Remember to expect nothing in return.

At times (usually few), the relationship can remain challenging, even toxic, despite your 100 percent commitment and self-discipline. When this occurs, you need to avoid being the **"Knower"** and shift to being the **"Learner."** Avoid Knower statements/thoughts like "that won't work," "I'm right, you are wrong," "I know it and you don't," "I'll teach you," "that's just the way it is," "I need to tell you what I know," etc.

Instead use Learner statements/thoughts like "Let me find out what is going on and try to understand the situation," "I could be wrong," "I wonder if there is anything of value here," "I wonder if...." etc. In other words, as a Learner, be curious!

PRINCIPLE PARADOX

This may strike you as strange, but here's the paradox: When you take authentic responsibility for a relationship, more often than not the other person quickly chooses to take responsibility as well. Consequently, the 100/0 relationship quickly transforms into something approaching 100/100. When that occurs, true breakthroughs happen for the individuals involved, their teams, their organizations, and their families.

EXPECT NOTHING

Expectations are something that you expect, not something to which you are entitled. Expectations are not required or guaranteed. As a matter of fact, parties in relationships are often unaware of each other's expectations. We're sometimes even unaware of our own expectations until they go unfulfilled!

Furthermore, when our expectations of others are negative, they can sometimes lead to a self-fulfilling prophecy, like when you find yourself thinking, "I can't believe I have to complete this project with Brian. He never contributes." In addition, our own behavior can begin to reinforce our negative expectation. We feel that Brian never contributes so we don't communicate with Brian or assign him important tasks. "See," we tell ourselves, "Brian really doesn't contribute. Just like I expected."

The 100/0 Principle asks that you take full responsibility for a relationship and expect nothing in return. This means that your relationships must take priority over your expectations. Failed expectations can derail great relationships when they cause:

Betrayal

Frustration

Resentfulness

Disappointment

Anger

Desire to abandon the relationship

THE 100/0 PRINCIPLE

ALLOWS YOU TO TAKE RESPONSIBILITY FOR YOUR RELATIONSHIPS WITHOUT BEING WEIGHED DOWN BY UNREALISTIC EXPECTATIONS. HAVING REALISTIC EXPECTATIONS OF OTHERS INVOLVES REALIZING THAT WE'RE ALL LESS THAN PERFECT.

Instead of looking for others to meet our needs, we must take responsibility for making relationships work. For most of us, shaping our behavior this way is counterintuitive and we need help navigating this path.

PLEASE READ ON!

Relate to It

WHEN HAVE YOU GIVEN MORE THAN YOU EXPECTED?

Your job, and mine, is to give more and expect less. When we do this, our hearts will be freed from negative judgment, and our happiness and effectiveness will multiply beyond what seems possible.

"The real beginning of influence comes as others sense you are being influenced by them—

When they feel understood by you—

that you have listened deeply and sincerely, and that you are open."

STEPHEN COVEY

CHAPTER 3

ALL

> *"People are lonely because
> they build walls instead of bridges."*

JOSEPH F. NEWTON

or

NOTHING

My mom used to say, "If you want to change someone, change your-self first." What my mom was saying was consistent with *The 100/0 Principle*. Most of us, however, are more familiar with a quite different notion . . . that a good relationship is based on a 50/50 proposition. I'll do my 50%, you agree to do your 50%, and we'll have a great relationship. The problem, of course, is that when something breaks down in the relation-ship, each person tends to blame the other— to point the finger as if it were the other person's fault.

A few years ago, a philosopher came up with a new relationship theory: the 100/100 proposition. It goes like this:

"I'll take 100% responsibility, you do the same, and we can't miss."

This looked good at first; however, in practice it had the same shortcoming as the 50/50 proposition, namely the blame game. The 100/100 idea has another inherent flaw: Each person has high, even unreal-istic expectations of the other. After all, each person expects the other to take full responsibility.

ROADBLOCKS TO 100/0

Jack Canfield, the co-author of the *Chicken Soup* series of books, has a favorite quote, "If we're not a little uncomfortable every day, we're not growing. All the good stuff is outside our comfort zone."

The roadblocks to effectively implementing *The 100/0 Principle* are captured in that quote. When we allow our automatic, knee-jerk tendencies to govern our relationships with others, we almost surely stay inside our comfort zone, and avoid the good stuff—the learning, the growth, the unprecedented results available to us.

Most often, the only roadblock to 100/0 is . . .

YOUR WILLINGNESS TO SUSPEND JUDGMENT AND TAKE **FULL RESPONSIBILITY** FOR THE RELATIONSHIP.

When you do this authentically, most of the time truly great things will happen. When they don't, here are some other things that might need addressing:

When the other person acts in a manner undeserving of your respect and kindness.

Be kind and respectful anyway. Choose your response.

When your friends and associates remind you of how wrong the other person is.

Remember, the relationship is more important than who is right or wrong. Think for yourself.

When the other person should know better.

This roadblock often occurs with people such as the so-called "toxic" boss. Today, more than ever, your boss needs your support. Bosses, like most people, are not as insensitive or nasty or heartless as they may seem. Break through the typical judgmental employee reaction and treat that boss with respect and kindness, even if they don't deserve it, and see what happens.

When the other person doesn't respond in kind.

Remember, The 100/0 Principle is all or nothing, and the all is on your part. You take full responsibility, expecting nothing in return. You accept the other person's feelings and responses. You become a learner, not a knower. You are persistent.

When you realize there are no guarantees.

The truth is there are no guarantees in The 100/0 Principle. *Sometimes it doesn't work. The great majority of the time it does. Give yourself permission to step into the breach, even when it's uncomfortable. You have a great deal to gain, and nothing to lose.*

A WORD OF CAUTION

There are some circumstances (thankfully, relatively few) where *The 100/0 Principle* does not apply. Examples include situations in which the other person's behavior is intolerable, such as lying, cheating, stealing or committing a crime. In those circumstances, that person's behavior would likely dictate actions on your part quite different from actions stemming from *The 100/0 Principle.*

Notwithstanding that word of caution, *The 100/0 Principle* has proven to be the simplest, most direct and most effective way to create solid relationships. Shift your thinking from "it takes two" to "I can and will create a relationship with that person." Take responsibility for the success of the relationship, expect nothing in return, and watch what happens!

Relate to It

THINK ABOUT YOUR MOST PRECIOUS MEMORIES. DO THEY INVOLVE THINGS OR PEOPLE?

The most important things in life aren't things at all; in fact, the most important things are the relationships you have with family, friends and others. Research has shown that people who just have things aren't very satisfied, while people who have many good relationships usually have a happy, successful life.

"Commitment to others is the stuff character is made of;

the power to change the face of things,
to create a new future."

ANONYMOUS

CHAPTER 4

"*Give every man thy ear
but few thy voice.*"

WILLIAM SHAKESPEARE

LISTEN TO
THIS

While our culture clearly emphasizes speaking over listening, listening is one of the most direct and powerful means to creating 100/0 relationships. It is also the foundation for great leadership, high-performance teams and effective organizations.

We've all felt, at some time or another, that we're not being heard. We've felt our comments have been dismissed, that our ideas aren't valid, that our efforts don't count. But those feelings don't really stem from not being heard.

THE REAL ISSUE IS THAT
someone was not listening.

Do you feel like having a relationship, of any kind, with someone who doesn't listen to you? Of course not. That's why listening is so important to relationships. If you want an effective, constructive relationship with someone, you need to listen to—not just hear—what they have to say.

AUTOMATIC **VS. CREATIVE** LISTENING

Most of us listen automatically, which takes two forms: not listening at all or listening judgmentally. Think about how you listen to someone you like vs. someone about whom you don't feel so fondly. You judge what the former is saying more favorably than you judge what the latter is saying.

THERE ARE OTHER MANNERS OF
AUTOMATIC LISTENING AS WELL:

Looking for a fatal flaw

Thinking about how to respond

Concluding what is being said is not valid

Assuming we already know the information

Trying to figure out how the information fits with
what we already know

With creative listening, on the other hand, you must determine who's in charge. Is it you or your automatic thoughts and responses? Either the conversations have you or you have the conversations.

The first step to becoming a creative listener is to be aware of your automatic listener . . . and hit the off button.

NOW THAT IT'S QUIET, ASK YOURSELF:

WHAT IS THE SPEAKER'S COMMITMENT?

WHAT ARE THE POSSIBILITIES?

WHAT CAN I LEARN?

WHAT IS THE SPEAKER'S REALITY?

WHAT ARE THE SPEAKER'S CONCERNS?

WHERE CAN WE ALIGN?

WHAT WILL WORK?

When we choose to listen creatively, we give people a genuine chance to be heard. We also offer our teams and organizations the chance to have true collaboration, communication, creativity, risk-taking and trust.

During a recent consulting engagement, a member of the company's senior leadership team asked if I could coach her on a problem she was having. I agreed and we met for an hour.

During the time we were together, I really listened to her concerns. Rather than offering advice, I simply acknowledged her concerns with an occasional "Uh-huh" or "I understand." I did a great deal of listening and very little talking. At the end of the hour she had reached a clear resolution to her problem. "That was the best conversation I've had in a long time," she told me. "I can't thank you enough."

ALL I DID WAS LISTEN.

Just like *The 100/0 Principle* takes real commitment and self-discipline, so does listening. Once you begin listening creatively, you'll find not only your communications will flourish, so will your relationships.

Creative listening is a piece, a very important piece, of giving 100 percent in your relationships.

4 Principles of Listening

LISTENING GRANTS OTHERS THE POWER OF SPEAKING.

LISTENING IS A GIFT. BE GENEROUS WITH IT.

WHAT WE LISTEN TO IS MORE IMPORTANT THAN WHAT WE SAY.

COMMUNICATION IS WHAT IS HEARD, NOT WHAT IS SAID.

WHY IS LISTENING SO DIFFICULT FOR SO MANY?

Here are some insights compiled by the International Listening Association:

—◆—

Most of us are distracted, preoccupied or forgetful
about 75% of the time we should be listening.

We listen at 125-250 words per minute,
but think at 1,000-3,000 words per minute.

Immediately after we listen to someone,
we only recall about 50% of what he or she said.

Long-term, we only remember 20% of what we hear.

—◆—

Listening has been identified as one of the top skills employers
seek in entry-level employees as well as those being promoted. More than
35 business studies indicate that listening is a top skill needed for success
in business.

Relate to It

HAVE A CONVERSATION WITH SOMEONE.

Take notice of your automatic listening, and then choose to listen creatively.

"Courage is
WHAT IT TAKES TO
STAND UP AND SPEAK;

Courage is also
WHAT IT TAKES TO
SIT DOWN AND LISTEN."

SIR WINSTON CHURCHILL

CHAPTER 5

IT'S NOT *who* YOU KNOW...

"*Assumptions are the termites of relationships.*"

HENRY WINKLER

IT'S *how* YOU KNOW THEM

k, so knowing the right people is important. But **how you know the people in your life, the way you relate to them**, is even more important.

TO FIND OUT HOW YOU KNOW SOMEONE,
ASK YOURSELF:

DO I JUDGE THIS PERSON?

DO I MAKE ASSUMPTIONS ABOUT THIS PERSON?

DO I EXPECT THINGS FROM THIS PERSON?

DO I LET THIS PERSON AFFECT HOW I ACT?

DO I PUT MY SUCCESS IN JEOPARDY BECAUSE I DO ALL OF THESE THINGS?

Before becoming a consultant, I had the privilege of working with Joe Sullivan, CEO of Swift and Company. Once or twice a year we held planning sessions off-site. Invariably, Joe would disappear shortly after we arrived at the hotel or conference center. But we always knew where to find him; he would be in a remote section of the facility talking with the janitor, security guard or another behind-the-scenes person.

Why? "Oh that's simple," he would say. "I like to ask questions and listen to those folks; they always teach me something. They often have a unique perspective on things and I learn a lot from them."

Joe used these experiences to implement a successful strategy at Swift called the "front-line management system," in which decision-making was pushed down to the lowest possible levels. He was confident it would work. He truly believed that those in the "front line" of any organization had more knowledge and ability than most people gave them credit for.

Within three years, Swift progressed from a break-even operation to the top third of the entire food industry in all meaningful profitability measures.

Joe Sullivan and others like him don't fall into the trap of allowing judgment to prematurely discredit the value of another person.

PUT DOWN YOUR GAVEL

To use *The 100/0 Principle* well, you'll need to keep in mind—and keep reminding yourself—that there is no room for judging others. If you're really going to take full responsibility for a relationship, your judgement isn't necessary.

When you judge someone, you're creating reality and you might rob yourself of some valuable lessons. If I hadn't put aside my judgment, I never would have learned from "Irish."

In the 1970s, my wife and I lived in an area called Tudor City, located near the United Nations plaza in New York City. In those days I played a lot of basketball on the outdoor court at the corner of 40th Street and FDR Drive.

Often there were several homeless people hanging around the court. At first I didn't pay attention to them; in fact, I hoped they would go away. I was afraid of them. I found them unappealing. They didn't leave, so over several weeks I started interacting with them. Their leader was a guy named "Irish."

As I got to know them, Irish and his friends shattered my image of the homeless. They may have been filthy on the outside, but they were pure of heart on the inside. They remain among the nicest, most considerate people I have ever known. Talking and shooting baskets with Irish and his pals became a highlight of my days.

What particularly impressed me was the exemplary team they formed. They were "all for one and one for all." Their fundamental commitment was to take care of each other—to literally help each other survive.

Irish and his friends demonstrated many characteristics of high-performance teams that years later became cornerstones of my consulting practice:

Willingness to take a stand
(in their case, for each other's survival)

Penchant for straight talk
(being open and honest)

Ability to align with each other
(fully support a decision, even in the face of dissention)

Ability to handle problems without being defeated

Their commitment to each other was beautiful to behold, and a great learning experience for me. Next time you feel inclined to judge someone, remember to put down your gavel and focus on your 100 percent of the relationship.

Relate to It

HAVE YOU EVER FELT JUDGED?

WHAT WAS YOUR RELATIONSHIP LIKE WITH THE PERSON WHO JUDGED YOU?

ARE YOU DAMAGING ANY RELATIONSHIPS BY JUDGING OTHERS?

"We can never judge the lives
of others, because each person knows
only their own pain and renunciation.
It's one thing to feel that you are on
the right path, but it's another to think
that yours is the only path."

PAULO COELHO

CHAPTER 6

IT REALLY

"No road is long with good company."

TURKISH PROVERB

WORKS!

When you try the *The 100/0 Principle*, the other party will respond in one of two ways: in kind, enabling the relationship to shift from 100/0 toward 100/100; or in the status quo, and the relationship will remain as is. There are no guarantees! In fact, that's one reason the principle is called "100/0" … you take full responsibility while expecting nothing in return and possibly getting nothing in return from the other person.

Notwithstanding the latter possibility,
there are two pieces of good news:

Most of the time the other person responds in kind, and the relationship shifts from 100/0 to something approaching 100/100.

The other piece of good news—even in the unlikely event the other person does not respond in kind—is that good things usually happen anyway.

The following story demonstrates that phenomenon.

*"A smile is the shortest distance
between two people."*

VICTOR BORGE

In a recent consulting engagement, I was asked to improve the relationship between two functional leaders—the senior vice president of sales and the senior vice president of administration. These two people had real animosity for each other, which rubbed off on their subordinates. Thus the company essentially had two important functions, or silos, where the people in each silo worked well with others in the same silo, but had difficulty working effectively with their counterparts in the other silo.

I knew that all leaders have an exponential impact on their people, so I endeavored to strengthen the relationship between the two leaders by coaching them to apply *The 100/0 Principle* with each other. One leader, the senior vice president of sales, quickly adopted the principle. The senior vice president of administration, however, refused to accept this principle and never materially changed his negative behavior toward the other leader.

Can you guess what happened? The people in the sales function, observing the new, positive behavior of their leader, began treating their counterparts in administration with grace and respect, expecting nothing in return. The administrative people, by and large, responded in kind, despite no tangible change by their leader.

The measurable results of the two functions and the entire company began to set all-time records. They will tell you that their strengthened relationships across the silos were the key to those record results. And this occurred despite an important person—the senior vice president of administration—not responding in kind to the positive actions of the vice president of sales.

GREAT THINGS HAPPEN WITH **THE 100/0 PRINCIPLE** EVEN WHEN THE OTHER PERSON DOES NOT RECIPROCATE. **THE GOOD NEWS: THE OTHER PERSON USUALLY RESPONDS FAVORABLY,** AS YOU'LL SEE FROM THE FOLLOWING STORIES.

TEACHERS INFLUENCE
ETERNITY

"GIVE LOVE TO
OTHER PEOPLE,
EVEN THOUGH THEY
DON'T DESERVE IT."

Dr. James MacDonald

When my wife, Barbara, my daughter Andrea, and I visited Washington, DC, recently we had the pleasure of meeting an Illinois Senator. Upon learning that Andrea is a teacher, the Senator replied, "I'm so glad you're a teacher because teachers influence eternity."

Andrea teaches at the Dieterich School in East Aurora, Illinois, where Principal Gwen Miller can teach us a lesson on *The 100/0 Principle*.

Principal Miller has a sign over her office door that reads, "Children need love, especially when they do not deserve it."* By all accounts, in her 38 years at Dieterich, Principal Miller has met and surpassed that standard. She recognizes that all students have strengths, even when only the weaknesses show. She insists all teachers find those strengths and build on them. During Andrea's first year of teaching, one of her students became surly and defiant, so she asked Mrs. Miller for help with that student. Mrs. Miller, in a gentle yet authoritarian tone told the student to stand up, walk quietly to the bathroom, and wash his face.

"Wake yourself up. When you come back, you and I will sit at a table out in the hallway and you will show me what a wonderful reader you are," requested Mrs. Miller. And that's exactly what happened.

Andrea says that one interaction between Mrs. Miller and the student resulted in the student's transformation. From that point on, he came to class demonstrating a whole new level of alertness, participation, and consistent, positive behavior.

Mrs. Miller took full responsibility for her relationship with that young man, and he stepped up to the plate and met her expectations.

NEXT TIME SOMEONE YOU'RE INTERACTING WITH DOESN'T DESERVE YOUR LOVE (OR RESPECT OR ATTENTION) GIVE IT TO THEM ANYWAY. GIVE THEM THE CHANCE TO STEP UP TO THE PLATE FOR YOU.

*Harold S. Hulbert

EDUCATION OF THE HEART

Mrs. Liz Hardy, another teaching colleague of my daughter Andrea, has taught first and second grade for over 30 years. Before the start of the 2009/2010 school year, she told a group of teachers, "Education of the heart of our students is just as important, if not more important, than the education of their mind."

One example: After daily recess on the playground, Mrs. Hardy has a 20-25 minute session with her whole class during which her students discuss how they related to each other and others from different classes while on the playground. Her students share what went well and what conflicts occurred. Then Mrs. Hardy discusses how the conflicts can be handled effectively and the students practice handling conflict through role play.

The bottom line for Mrs. Hardy is helping her kids care about each other and establish lasting relationships. Mrs. Hardy seems to never have behavioral problems in her class. Her students are always calm, quiet and polite. What a great learning environment Mrs. Hardy creates.

"SOME PEOPLE COME INTO OUR LIVES AND LEAVE FOOTPRINTS
ON OUR HEARTS AND WE ARE NEVER EVER THE SAME."

Flavia Weedn

Mrs. Hardy is a celebrity in East Aurora. When she runs into former students, their faces light up in sheer joy to see her again. Hugs abound all around, no matter what the age. The legacy of Mrs. Hardy is impossible to dismiss. She is a shining example of Roland Burris' comment that "teachers influence eternity."

Mrs. Hardy loves her students unconditionally—the epitome of *The 100/0 Principle*.

BEING THE 100

"TRUE DISCOVERY CONSISTS NOT IN FINDING NEW LANDSCAPES,
BUT IN SEEING THE SAME LANDSCAPE WITH NEW EYES."

Marcel Proust

When I was the chief financial officer of a Fortune 500 consumer goods company, I reported to the company's president as well as the CFO of our parent company. I did not like the CFO, and I'm quite sure the feeling was mutual. My immediate boss (Jack, my company's president) got wind of this, and one day gave me a surprising directive:

"Al, I want you to immediately create a relationship with Paul—it's your most important short-term goal and I am counting on you to do it."

"Jack," I responded, "that's the hardest thing you could ask me to do. Do you really mean it?"

"I sure do," he answered.

"You mean I should create a business relationship, don't you?" I inquired.

"I mean a relationship, period," Jack answered. "And if you can create a great relationship with Paul, all the better."

Well, I didn't like it, but the directive was crystal clear. Jack was telling me I was to be the "100" in a 100/0 relationship with Paul.

I didn't know what to do at first, but then it struck me that I should simply treat Paul with the same decency and respect with which I treated others. And even though it was uncomfortable at first, that's exactly what I did.

Guess what happened? Almost immediately, Paul began to respond to me in kind; the very behavior that initially caused me to dislike him disappeared. We went on to have a strong relationship for the two years we continued working together. *The 100/0 Principle* served me well in a work situation where it was important for two people to work together effectively.

As a business coach, I almost always use *The 100/0 Principle* with my clients. In a recent engagement, an investment team adopted the principle in working with each other. As their team chemistry and rapport grew, their investment results grew commensurately!

BREAKTHROUGH ON THE
HOME
FRONT

"ARE WE NOT LIKE TWO VOLUMES OF ONE BOOK?"

Marceline Desbordes-Valmore

My mom, who passed away a few years ago, was an admirable person in many ways. However, during the first few years of our marriage, my wife, Barbara, and I often became upset with her numerous "digs" about our lifestyle. Our upset finally triggered a confrontation with my mom and dad, and we didn't see them for a year. Fortunately, Barbara saw the error of our ways; she made me realize our relationship with my mom was more important than who was right or wrong.

I will never forget the phone call to my mom after a year of not speaking. I asked her to forgive Barbara and me, and I told her I was glad that she and dad were my parents. I told her we were fine except for missing her, and asked if we could come for a visit. As I was talking, I felt the phone line between Chicago and Florida expand to an infinite width, symbolic of our new acceptance of each other.

Barbara and I quickly went to visit my parents. On the way there, we made a pact to not let anything anyone said upset us. Although my mom made a few of her familiar "digs," we responded without anger. "You know, Mom," we'd say, "we'll really think about that." Or even, "You're probably right."

Until my mom's death 10 years later, we enjoyed a truly great relationship. I had a mom again. For those 10 years, we can't recall hearing one "dig" from her—another example of *The 100/0 Principle* leading to a 100/100 relationship.

TOUGH *Love*

Although the "toxic" boss can be very difficult, bosses aren't the only people who can throw a wrench into our happiness. Sometimes, relationships with those closest to us—like parents, children and other family members—are most in need of *The 100/0 Principle*.

What if one of your children was 25 years old and addicted to alcohol or drugs? For the last six years, you have tried everything to help your daughter, but to no avail. In fact, your daughter is now in her fourth rehabilitation center, with the distinct possibility of being sent to prison for two felonies. As most parents would, you have taken 100% responsibility, but with zero to show for it. Zero means expect nothing, and nothing is what you've generated. This is your daughter. You love her unconditionally. You want the absolute best for her.

What would you do?

If you're like most parents, you will continue for as long as it takes to try to help her. You will do almost anything to help her out of the mess she's created. Unfortunately, it probably won't be good enough. What is often required is a profound commitment to non-judgment, the under-pinning of *The 100/0 Principle*. Thus, parents must take on a profoundly expanded empathy for their daughter (meaning profound acceptance of the "0" in *The 100/0 Principle*). The parental empathy in this situation means profound acceptance, without judgment of both the situation and the likely outcome. This non-judgmental empathy is, for most parents, extremely difficult—sometimes it means getting new help; often it means letting go and hoping/praying for the daughter to somehow, on her own, make a new choice in the direction of her life.

Most parents, left to their natural inclination, will automatically reject both the current behavior and the likely outcome. The alternative, as *The 100/0 Principle* suggests, is for the parents to accept the truth without judgment, and do whatever it takes, including the difficult coun-terintuitive step of letting go as a conscious choice.

People are People
IT'S AS SIMPLE AS THAT!

People who travel the world over, like my friend Sam Schotsky, will tell you that people are people. Despite cultural, religious and other differences, people are essentially the same as you and me, whether living next door to us or on the other side of the world.

Over lunch in Chicago recently, Sam, who was born in New York and lived most of his life in Los Angeles, told me of experiences he's had doing business in Saudi Arabia, Kuwait and Dubai:

On long flights from New York to Saudi Arabia, all the passengers were always casually dressed. Just before landing in Saudi Arabia, all the Arab women covered themselves completely, as required by their culture.

Sam's business partner in Saudi Arabia was a Muslim, and prayed five times a day in a mosque.

The business partner's wife, also a Muslim, could not speak to Sam in any public setting, including in a car. She did, however, speak to Sam when he was at their house for dinner.

That was it! That's all Sam said. That's what Sam relayed to me during our lunch. No conclusion, no judgment on Sam's part. After several moments of silence, I asked Sam, "What do you make of all that?" His response was, "Pretty interesting, don't you think?" That's all he said! I then asked Sam how the business partnership turned out over there—was it successful or not?

Sam's answer, "Tremendously successful—maybe the most successful experience I've had in my 35 years in business. People are people! It's as simple as that."

Sam's story reminds me of a *Business Week* article about Natalia Paruz, who plays the musical saw in New York subway stations. Natalia says her music recently managed to get a Christian family, a Jewish family and a Muslim family into a conversation. Natalia says, "If people can relate on a personal level like that—then there is hope that world peace might be possible after all."

Sam's story is another successful example of how well things can go for us when we act without judgment and expectation. Think how differently Sam's outcome would have been if he had judged his business partners and their customs, or if he had expected them to behave differently.

UN**CONDITIONAL**
Acceptance

"KEEP DOING OUTRAGEOUSLY
GENEROUS AND LOVING THINGS TO OTHERS."

Ray Carter

My wife, Barbara, and I have been married for 38 years. From the first time we dated, Barbara demonstrated *The 100/0 Principle*. Her 100% responsibility, including great kindness, was especially evident in the way she was able to create acceptance in difficult roommate situations. Several of the people she lived with in those days had what most of us would call "annoying tendencies." Occasionally, others' judgments of those tendencies led to near conflict … until Barbara stepped in. She saw those annoyances as simply part of the human condition and would say, "Oh, that's just the way she is; isn't she funny when she does that?" Usually, Barbara would completely diffuse the issue and enable all the roommates to live in peace and harmony. She accepted people the way they were.

Barbara's admirable quality of accepting others was really put to the test when our daughter Ashley, who has Down syndrome, was born in 1980. Barbara knew she needed to see Ashley the way she saw others—with unconditional acceptance. But at first, she had great difficulty in doing that; she couldn't see the good in Ashley. In fact, she only saw the disability and the retardation. The question Barbara asked herself was, "How can I apply what I have done for years with my own daughter?"

The answer was a lot of hard work on Barbara's part. For 15 months, Barbara was in therapy. She also took Est training, which helped her see Ashley as a potentially great gift, rather than a burden. About the same time, she also became a Christian, which led to her achieving unconditional love for Ashley. This process of growth was not an easy one for Barbara, but she's the first one to tell you how valuable that process was.

Taking 100% responsibility for a relationship is not always easy and takes some hard work, as Barbara's experience demonstrates. But the outcome is so worthwhile.

That quality of Barbara's—to accept people the way they are—helped create solid relationships and remains to this day. In fact, I have a strong hunch that our 38-year marriage has endured in large measure thanks to Barbara's acceptance of my many "annoying tendencies" over the years.

"S*My*Second" *parents*

"IT'S ALL ABOUT PEOPLE. PEOPLE MATTER MOST. EVERYBODY COUNTS."

Dr. Joe Stowell

My good friends, Ann and Floyd Grieve, have been much more than that over the years ... they have been my "second" parents, and epitomized *The 100/0 Principle*.

During my freshman year at the University of Connecticut, I quickly became a friend of Dick Grieve, Ann and Floyd's son. One weekend Dick, or "Glump" as we all called him, invited five or six of his fellow freshmen, including me, to go with him to visit his parents who lived about 30 miles from campus. All of us resisted Glump's invitation. After all, here we were in our first year of college, having finally severed those direct ties to parents. We were on our own, and we could think of a lot of things we'd rather do than spend a weekend with someone's parents. But Glump was a great guy, and somehow enrolled all of us to go with him.

That weekend, every one of us had a terrific time with Glump's parents and his Grandma. They were unconditionally accepting and gracious to each of us. They seemed to have absolutely no judgment. We were who we were, and that was fine with them. Over the ensuing four years of college, all of us visited Ann, Floyd and Grandma numerous times. We often said there was no place we would rather be.

I soon learned that everyone who met Ann, Floyd and Grandma loved them almost instantly. One example: One day while I was visiting them, Floyd and Ann were asked to look after the 16-year-old son of one of their friends during dinner. During that two-hour dinner, that boy was transformed. He arrived at Ann and Floyd's house as an introverted, isolated, sullen teenager. By the time dinner was over, he was a laughing, warm-hearted, outgoing individual. What a change! I couldn't believe what was happening before my eyes. When he arrived that day, Ann, Floyd and Grandma were able to get on his level. He was accepted by them just the way he was, and he knew that almost immediately. They asked him questions, really listened to him, and did a lot of laughing together. During dinner, he was made to feel like one of the family, accepted with grace, warmth and kindness. Ann, Floyd and Grandma were truly unique and special people.

After college graduation, I lived with Ann and Floyd twice—before and after my two-year Army commitment. (My real parents were overseas on a business assignment.) Ann and Floyd became my "second" parents then, and continue in that role to this day. And Glump continues to be my best friend. Additionally, Glump and his wife, Diana, have opened their home to many people over the years, part of the enduring great legacy of Ann and Floyd, and Grandma too. They consistently practiced *The 100/0 Principle* every day of their lives. They made the world a better place for all of us.

NEXT TIME SOMEONE COMES INTO YOUR LIFE . . .

try accepting them unconditionally,

with absolutely no judgment.

Expect nothing from them.

Take 100% responsibility for the relationship.

Act as if your life depends upon it.

You'll give them the gift of acceptance and who knows what you'll receive in return!

Relate to It

DO YOU THINK PEOPLE ARE WRONG WHEN THEY DON'T LOOK OR ACT THE WAY YOU EXPECT?

Choose to act differently ... accept people for who they are.

CHAPTER 7

IT DOESN'T T

"*I want people to be more open and more tolerant. I want them to know that behind every stranger is a backstory that is the common denominator—for we all share in the human experience: pain, sadness, grief, lack of love, and then, with hope and help, step by step achievements.*"

OPRAH WINFREY

AKE TWO TO

TANGO

You're probably familiar with the old adage, "It takes two to tango." But to have happier, more productive relationships, you've got to stop dancing. *The 100/0 Principle* is the simplest, most direct and most effective way to create solid relationships that will benefit you both personally and professionally.

While it may take two to tango, it only takes you to commit to creating a relationship with the people in your life. Take full responsibility for your relationships and consciously choose to suspend judgment of people. Indeed, treat them with respect and dignity, whether deserved or not.

Think about to whom you can apply *The 100/0 Principle*. Almost all parents easily and naturally have a 100/0 relationship with their children and grandchildren—a state of unconditional love. Parents might not love how their children behave, but regardless of the tantrums and stubbornness, the fits and idiosyncrasies, at the end of the day, parents still have a fierce love for their children.

Most of us also have 100/0 relationships with our close friends. Our friends have proven themselves to us, so it's fairly easy for us to take full responsibility for our friendships in good times or bad.

It's in the other important relationships in my life, and probably yours too, where our track record needs improvement:

MARRIAGE. The divorce rate in the United States has been around 50% for a long time. Yet research has shown that virtually all marriages have challenges. Why does one person stay with a challenging marriage, while another looks for happiness in another mate? Certainly one valid explanation is *The 100/0 Principle*—whether someone chooses to take real responsibility for the relationship rather than depending on a marriage partner as a primary source of happiness. Remember that no one can make you happy; happiness is a response that you choose.

EXTENDED FAMILY. Brothers, sisters, in-laws, aunts, uncles, cousins, nieces, nephews. Most of us tend to have a spotty record here too. We tend to forget that our family members are the only ones we have—my Aunt Edna is my only Aunt Edna. It behooves me to create and sustain a relationship with her, and with my other extended family members too.

What someone allegedly said or did to someone else 10 years ago shouldn't impact your happiness today. It's your choice whether you let it or not. When you hold on to ill feelings you're victimizing yourself. Let it go and take responsibility for making a positive future. You're in charge of you and your actions.

COWORKERS, CUSTOMERS, SUPPLIERS. All the research, plus my 20 years as a consultant to thousands of business people, proves without a doubt that the success of an individual, a team or an entire organization depends largely on the quality of the relationships. Remember, actions + relationships = results. When it comes to your coworkers, customers and suppliers, practice 100/0. Take responsibility for those relationships, period.

PEOPLE YOU MEET. As we've discussed previously, we tend to automatically react in a judgmental manner when we meet others. *The 100/0 Principle* is the antithesis to judgment. It's about deciding that you are in charge, not your automatic tendencies.

Of course, with people we don't know, some caution is in order. However, we tend to exercise caution even when not warranted, such as with people who look or act differently, speak a different language, or have a physical or mental disability.

My friend Roger Breisch, a very wise person, once told me, "When you attend any social gathering, look for the person you least likely would want to meet. Then go over and introduce yourself—you will likely be surprised by how much you learn, and be blessed by the interaction." Well said, Roger!

Similarly, I urge you to give yourself permission to approach people who are different from you, including people with mental and/or physical disabilities. You will likely feel uncomfortable. Choose to be willing to feel uncomfortable, then appreciate what a great choice you made and congratulate yourself for making that choice. What once was your least likely choice of action will become your most likely choice. Congratulations!

THE DIFFICULT BOSS. In my speeches about *The 100/0 Principle*, the Q&A sessions at the end often include "The Toxic Boss." It seems that everyone has had at least one toxic boss. Unfortunately, many people have had more than one.

The questions I'm asked usually go something like this:

"I have had a toxic boss for a long time, and nothing I've tried has made any difference. He (or she) is as toxic as ever, and will never change. How does The 100/0 Principle *apply to this?"*

My first response is that the use of the word "toxic" (which means "poisonous") likely defeats any chance of creating a relationship. Extensive research has shown that the language we use literally creates our world— our thoughts and language influence our lives and our relationships. The words we use profoundly shape our thinking and actions. My advice is to drop the word "toxic" and say "difficult" boss instead.

I always share the following story. It perfectly illustrates how I was finally able to think and act using *The 100/0 Principle*.

THE
TOXIC
BOSS TRAP

"Patience is the companion of wisdom."

Many of us, at some time, have complained about a difficult boss. They are the bosses no one likes; their existence almost seems toxic as they infiltrate and pervade teams, projects and companies. Those of us who have, or have had, toxic bosses allow our negative judgment to diminish our responsibility for the relationship. We think they are wrong and should know better. They're the bosses, after all. We also receive confirmation from our associates about how wrong the boss is, which doesn't help. At best, we make a half-hearted attempt at the relationship. And we usually give up too soon.

I experienced four difficult bosses during my 18-year corporate career. With the first three, I made wrong choices—avoiding them as much as possible, complaining a lot, and relishing my co-workers' affirmations that I was so right and the boss was so wrong. My behavior did nothing to help my situation, nor did it help other people in the company. In fact, the first two times I encountered a difficult boss, I quit the company in anger. My harsh, negative judgment of my third difficult boss led to me being fired!

The fourth time, I finally got it right. He was probably the most "toxic" of them all. His modus operandi was to look good, not necessarily to do good. He treated others harshly, often with disrespect. But I refused to fall into the "toxic boss" trap, and committed to treating him with the dignity and respect I usually reserved for people I liked.

My team and I had a good relationship with him for the two years we worked for him. We refused to get "hooked" by his unusual behavior. We met regularly to discuss what we could do as a team to fulfill our 100% commitment to our relationship with him. And although any observer would agree he didn't change much during the two years we worked for him, our 100% responsibility for our relationship with him helped us support him and the company much more effectively. As I look back on that experience, I can't think of one person outside of our team who was as willing and able to take 100% responsibility for a relationship with him.

My team at that time consisted of six people. Five of us were promoted just after our stint with the difficult boss. All five of us were told that our ability to work with the difficult boss not only was important in its own right, but also enabled us to demonstrate our skills and become recognized for the right reasons. The bottom line—taking 100% responsibility with our "toxic" boss earned us significant promotions.

My relationship (or more accurately, the lack thereof) with my first three difficult bosses remains, 25 years later, a source of embarrassment for me. My hope is you don't make the same mistakes, and instead commit to the kind of relationship I had, along with my team, with boss number four.

By taking 100% responsibility for your professional relationships, you'll be able to serve your customers, your team, your boss and your company the best you can.

Any problem you have with another, as you know by now, has less to do with that person, and more to do with our deep expectations of him or her. Those expectations, of course, fly in the face of *The 100/0 Principle*, where the "0" calls for no expectations.

With anyone you encounter—from family and friends to colleagues and acquaintances—awareness and choice are extremely important. We must be aware of our biases, our emotions, our expectations; then we must consciously make a choice to respond with grace and kindness.

Finally, we must fully embrace the "0" and expect nothing in return. Usually, the other person will respond positively, but sometimes you actually get nothing in return. That's okay. You haven't lost anything. Your grace and kindness have likely helped you, your team or family, and your organization in ways that, at least initially, aren't readily apparent.

Relate to It

THINK ABOUT THE "0s" YOU'VE ENCOUNTERED. WERE YOU THE "100"?

In the 100/0 process, even when the "0" won't budge, somehow good things seem to happen anyway—things we can't see, at least initially, and things we can't predict.

CHAPTER 8

THE NEW

"Be kind, tender-hearted and forgiving to one another."

TY GOOCH

While it's wise to learn from experience, it is even wiser to learn from the experience of others. My objective in writing this book is exactly that—for you to learn from the stories and examples depicted in this book and, most importantly, for them to drive your actions as you implement *The 100/0 Principle* in your relationships. Let's take a look at the new 100% you.

It used to be like this; when you thought about a particular person, or saw that person coming toward you, your negative judgment kicked in. This response was so natural for you that you just let it happen. But now, you know your relationship with that person is more important than how right you are and how wrong he or she is.

You are conscious, you are ***aware*** of your automatic tendency to judge, so you ***choose*** to respond differently—with grace and kindness. You may have to consciously choose this new way of responding; soon it will become a helpful habit. Actively refraining from judgment won't be comfortable, especially at first, but you choose to do it anyway. You know the other person may not respond in kind—after all, there is no guarantee others will ever respond with anything but "0"—but you give 100% anyway.

You know that, in most cases, 100/0 becomes 100/100, because when you step up your efforts, the other person is likely to do the same.

This fact doesn't drive your actions, nor does it always happen quickly, but when it does, relationships can soar to new heights. It can happen for you, the other person, your team (or family) and your organization.

You are patient and persistent, too. You don't give up. Even when your patience and persistence does not lead to a 100/100 relationship, somehow, good things tend to happen in the relationship anyway. The 100% you give seems to reflect back on you and others.

Tips for Making Every Relationship Great:

WRITE IT DOWN

Develop the habit of writing down action steps describing exactly what you will do to enhance the relationship. Include what will be done, who will do it (in this case, you), and by when.

BE PATIENT AND PERSISTENT

Roadblocks will occur as you use *The 100/0 Principle*. So be patient and be persistent. Take full responsibility for your relationships and reject the temptation to give up and return to the status quo.

TAKE CONTROL

Stop asking, "Who's going to meet my needs?" and start asking, "Whose needs can I meet?" Think more about others than about yourself. This idea flies in the face of our natural tendency to be self absorbed. So give yourself permission to be uncomfortable as you implement *The 100/0 Principle*. When people contribute to others, they are more satisfied and deeply fulfilled.

EXPECT NOTHING

A major cause of upset in any domain of life is thwarted expectations. We typically have expectations of how others will act or what they will do. Sometimes those expectations are explicit, such as a clear request for the other person to do something; sometimes the expectations are implicit, that is, unspoken and assumed. Either way, when our expectations of another are not met, we're angry or upset. Thwarted expectations are probably the biggest barrier to strong relationships. *The 100/0 Principle*, by definition, mitigates or even eliminates this problem. Since I don't have any expectations of you, I won't be disappointed or upset no matter what you do or don't do.

FORM NEW HABITS

When you practice the above tips, you form new habits. You get good at
The 100/0 Principle without really thinking about it. These character-building
habits can lead to true mastery—mastery of what really counts in life. As you
practice it, a life-long habit will be formed, your discomfort will disappear,
and your life will be positively changed forever.

A Note About

LOVING OTHER PEOPLE

"Love means I care about what you care about."

DR. JOE STOWELL

The Bible says we should love other people ... all others. In fact, we should make relationships our number one priority. The good book says relationships are what life is all about. As Mother Teresa said, "It's not what you do, but how much love you put into it that matters."

Some years ago, I remember seeing a noteworthy cartoon on this subject in *Time* or *Newsweek*. The picture showed an elderly man on his deathbed, with family, friends and a media person gathered around. The caption read something like this:

> **MEDIA PERSON:**
> "What would you have done differently in your life if you could live it over again?"
>
> **DYING MAN:**
> "I would have realized much earlier in my life that relationships are what life is all about. I would have learned and acted on that truth much sooner, and given much less attention to achievements and acquisitions."

Most of us act similarly. We act as if relationships are something we are obligated to squeeze into our busy schedules, as if finding time for people in our lives is just one of our many tasks. Relationships are a low priority. We let our busyness get in the way of our relationships.

The truth is this: Loving other people is what life is all about. The important questions for you and me are: How do I treat other people? Do I judge them? Do I have unrealistic expectations for them? *The 100/0 Principle* includes several great gifts we can (in fact, we must) give to others:

The gift of *time*

The gift of *listening*

The gift of *graciousness and respect*

The gift of *laughter*

The gift of a *smile*

The 100/0 Principle requires us to place our full attention on others, not ourselves. You can begin *The 100/0 Principle* in your life right now, by taking responsibility for the success of a relationship. Think of a relationship in which you are not fully satisfied (for example, an individual from whom you are not getting the level of cooperation you would like).

ASK YOURSELF THESE QUESTIONS:

1. Determine if you are trying to be right about something, and if so, what?

2. Are you indeed right about this issue? What are others telling you about how right you are?

3. Decide if you are more interested in making the relationship work than in being right.

4. If you decide that the relationship is more important, decide what actions you will take, by when, to improve the relationship.

Relate to It

Relationships need to be your first priority. To accomplish that, I request you answer three questions:

WHO SHOULD YOU SPEND MORE TIME WITH?

WHAT WILL YOU CUT OUT OF YOUR SCHEDULE TO MAKE THAT POSSIBLE?

WHAT OTHER SACRIFICES WILL YOU MAKE?

"When we show love and compassion
in simple,
practical ways,
we are part of God's ministry to His people."

CINDY HESS KASPER

CHAPTER 9

IT
TAKES

"We are all in this together; we are not nearly as right as we think we are and others are not nearly as wrong as we would like to believe."

PAT BAILEY

HEART

The *100/0 Principle* changes peoples' lives. It leads to success and happiness for all involved.

Although it is not intuitive or natural for most of us, it is not rocket science either.

Any of us can do it.

The 100/0 Principle is about the heart, not so much about the head. Great selling, great customer service, great family and coworker relationships, great friendships and, as we've seen, great leadership, all comes primarily from the heart. In fact, in nearly every domain of our lives, if we have in our hearts the desire to serve others, we will be effective.

It's fundamentally about choosing to place our attention on others instead of on ourselves. It's choosing to take full, 100% responsibility for our relationships with others by extending grace and kindness unconditionally. The old saying is true: If you want to change someone, change yourself first. Take responsibility for the relationship working, expect nothing in return, and watch what happens!

WE ALL CAN DO THIS.
THE 100/0 PRINCIPLE IS A GREAT
GIFT ALL OF US CAN GIVE TO
OTHERS, AND IN SO DOING, MAKE
OUR WORLD A BETTER PLACE.
BY IMPLEMENTING THE 100/0
PRINCIPLE, YOU WILL MAKE YOUR
ROLE IN THIS WORLD INFINITELY
MORE EFFECTIVE, SATISFYING
AND SUCCESSFUL.

**YOU CAN DO IT! START RIGHT NOW.
IT'S YOUR CHOICE.**

AL RITTER is a management consultant and professional speaker, in addition to being an author. He is founder and president of The Ritter Consulting Group, and has consulted for the past 20 years with thousands of people across many industries in both the U.S. and overseas. Al is a leadership coach who works with CEOs, other leaders and teams committed to achieving breakthrough results both in their own and their organization's performance.

Before starting his own firm, Al worked for the consulting firm Accenture, where he was recognized as that firm's resident expert in leadership, team development, culture and large scale change. Earlier, he had a noteworthy corporate career, including senior vice president for Citigroup, chief financial officer for Swift & Company, and marketing and operations positions with PepsiCo.

Al is also the author of the book, *Life is a Paradox*, which demonstrates that the most important lessons in life, work and sports are often counter-intuitive—that is, they are not readily apparent and often conflict with our expectations.

As a professional speaker, Al speaks on leadership with businesses, associations and universities. He has delivered over 500 speeches, workshops and seminars.

Al holds an MBA from the Amos Tuck School of Dartmouth College, and played basketball and baseball for The University of Connecticut. He currently participates in triathlons.

He lives in Geneva, Illinois, with his wife, Barbara. They have two adult daughters.

Al can be reached at ahritter@ritterconsultinggroup.com

The
simple truths®
DIFFERENCE

For more information, please visit us at:
www.simpletruths.com

Simple Truths Philosophy

There is one thing in life that took me a long time to learn, and that's ... less is almost always more. This "simple truth" is the foundation on which our company was built. I wanted to create beautiful gift books that anyone can read in less than thirty minutes.

❖

If you have enjoyed this book we invite you to check out our entire collection of gift books, with free inspirational movies, at **www.simpletruths.com.**
You'll discover it's a great way to inspire *friends* and *family,* or to thank your best *customers* and *employees.*

We would love to hear how Simple Truths books enrich your life and others around you. Please send your comments to:

Simple Truths Feedback
1952 McDowell Road, Suite 300
Naperville, IL 60563
Or e-mail us at: comments@simpletruths.com

Or call us toll free…
800-900-3427